850

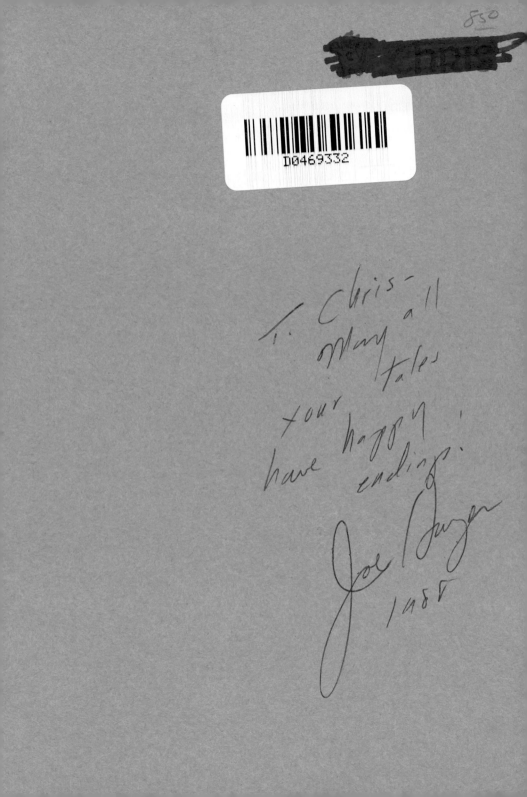

To Chris—
May all
your tales
have happy
endings.

Joe Bruzer
1988

The
Day
It
Snowed
Tortillas

Tales from Spanish New Mexico
retold by Joe Hayes

Illustrations & Design by Lucy Jelinek

A Mariposa Book

Published by
Mariposa Publishing
922 Baca Street
Santa Fe, New Mexico 87501
(505) 988-5582

FOURTH PRINTING 1986
FIRST PRINTING 1982

Selections from "The Day It Snowed Tortillas,"
"Coyote &," and "The Checker Playing Hound Dog"
by Joe Hayes available on cassette tapes from
Trails West Publishing, P.O. Box 8619,
Santa Fe, New Mexico, 87504-8619.

ISBN   0 933553-00-5

for Kathi and Adam

Table of Contents

The Day It Snowed
Tortillas

Here is a story about a poor woodcutter. He was very good at his work. He could swing his ax powerfully and cut down big trees. He would split them up into firewood to sell in the village. He made a good living.

But the poor man was not well educated. He couldn't read or write. He wasn't very bright either. He was always doing foolish things. But he was lucky. He had a very clever wife, and she would get him out of trouble.

One day he was working far off in the mountains, and when he started home at the end of the day, he saw three leather bags by the side of the trail.

He picked up the first bag and discovered that it was full of gold coins! He looked into the second. It was full of gold too. And so was the third.

He loaded the bags onto his donkey and took them home to show to his wife. She was aghast. "Don't tell anyone you found this gold!" she warned him. "It must belong to some robbers who have hidden it out in the mountains. If they find out we have it, they'll kill us to get it back!

But then she thought, "My husband! He can never keep a secret. What shall I do?"

She came up with a plan. She told her husband, "Before you do anything else, go into the village and

9

get me a sack of flour. I need a big sack. Bring me a hundred pounds of flour."

The man went off to the village grumbling to himself, "All day I work in the mountains, and now I have to drag home a hundred pounds of flour. I'm tired of all this work." But he bought the flour and brought it home to his wife.

"Thank you," she told him. "Now, you've been working awfully hard. Why don't you go lie down for a while?" He liked that idea. He lay down on the bed and soon fell fast asleep.

As soon as her husband began to snore, the woman went to work. She began to make tortillas. She made batch after batch of tortillas. She made them until the stack reached clear up to the ceiling in the kitchen. She turned that whole hundred pounds of flour into tortillas. Then she took them outside and threw them all over the ground.

The woodcutter was so tired he slept all that evening and on through the night. He didn't wake up until morning. When he awoke, he stepped outside and saw that the ground was covered with tortillas. He called to his wife. "What's the meaning of this?" he asked.

His wife joined him at the door. "Oh, my goodness! It must have snowed tortillas last night!"

"Snowed tortillas? I've never heard of such a thing."

"What? You've never heard of it snowing tortillas? Well! You're not very well educated. You'd better go to school and learn something."

So she packed him a lunch and dressed him up and made him go off to school.

He didn't know how to read or write, so they put him in the first grade. He had to squeeze into one of the little chairs the children sat in. The teacher asked questions and the children raised their hands enthusiastically. He didn't know the answers to any of those questions. He grew more and more embarrassed.

Then he had to go to the black board and write. He didn't even know the alphabet. The little boy beside him began to write his name on the board, and the woodcutter tried to copy the boy's letters. When the other children saw the man writing the boy's name instead of his own, they began to laugh at him.

He couldn't stand it any longer. He stomped out of the school and hurried home. He seized his ax. "I've had enough education," he told his wife. "I'm going to go cut firewood."

"Fine," she called after him. "You go do your work."

About a week later, just as the woman had suspected, the robbers showed up at the house one day. "Where is that gold your husband found?" they demanded.

The wife acted innocent. "Gold?" She shook her head. "I don't know anything about any gold."

"Come on!" the robbers said. "Your husband's been telling everyone in the village he found three sacks of gold. They belong to us. You'd better give them back."

She looked disgusted. "Did my husband say that?

Oh, that man! He says the strangest things! I don't know anything about your gold."

"That's a likely story. We'll find out. We'll wait here until he comes home." So the robbers waited around all day—sharpening their knives and cleaning their pistols.

Toward evening the woodcutter came up the trail with his donkey. The robbers ran out and grabbed him roughly. "Where's that gold you found?"

The woodcutter scratched his head. "Gold?" he mumbled. "Oh, yes. Now I remember. My wife hid it." He called out, "Wife, what did you do with that gold?"

His wife sounded puzzled. "What gold? I don't know what you're talking about."

"Sure you do. Don't you remember? It was just the day before it snowed tortillas. I came home with three bags of gold. And in the morning you sent me to school."

The robbers looked at one another. "Did he say, 'snowed tortillas'?" they whispered. "She sent him to school?" They shook their heads in dismay. "Why did we waste our time with this numbskull? He's out of his head!"

And they went away thinking the woodcutter was crazy and had just been talking a lot of nonsense.

From that day on, it didn't really matter whether he was well educated or clever. It didn't even matter if he was a good woodcutter. For he was a rich man. He and his wife had those three sacks of gold all to themselves. And the robbers never came back.

Pedro and Diablo

Once in a small mountain village there lived two men who were good friends. The one man's name was Pedro. The other? Well—no one remembered his name. You see, no one ever called him by his name. Instead, they used his nickname.

Back when he was only seven or eight years old, everyone had started calling him El Diablo—The Devil—because he was so mischievous.

In school, if there was some prank being played on the teacher, you could bet that El Diablo thought the whole thing up. He would get all the other boys involved, and they'd all get caught and get in trouble. So most of the boys learned to stay away from El Diablo. But not his good friend Pedro.

All the way through the grades and on up through high school El Diablo kept dragging his friend Pedro into trouble. And even when they were grown men and should have known better it was still happening. El Diablo was leading Pedro astray.

For example, there was the time that El Diablo said to his friend, "Pedro, have you noticed the apples on Old Man Martinez' tree? They look wonderful. Let's go steal some tonight. There's no moon. No one will see us."

Pedro said, "Oh, no! Old Man Martinez has that big dog. He'll bite my leg off!"

But El Diablo told him, "Don't worry about that dog. He keeps him inside at night. Come on. Let's get some apples." And he talked his friend into it.

That night the two friends got a big gunny sack and crept into Old Man Martinez' yard. They filled that sack with apples, then slipped back out onto the road.

Pedro whispered, "We'll have to find some place to divide these apples up."

Of course El Diablo had a great idea. "I know. We'll go to the *camposanto*, to the graveyard. Nobody will bother us there!"

So they went down the road until they came to the cemetery. They went in through the gate and walked along the low adobe wall that surrounded the graveyard until they found a dark, shadowy place right next to the wall.

They sat down and dumped out the apples and started to divide them into two piles. As they divided the apples, they whispered, "One for Pedro—one for Diablo... One for Pedro—one for Diablo...," making two piles of apples.

Now, it just so happened that a couple of men from the village had been out living it up that night—dancing and celebrating and drinking a little too much. In fact, they had got so drunk they couldn't make it home. They had fallen asleep leaning against that wall right over from where Pedro and El Diablo were dividing up the apples.

The one man was a big, round, fat fellow. The other was old and thin, with a face that was dry and withered looking.

A few minutes later, the old man woke up. From the other side of the wall, over in the graveyard, he heard a voice saying, "One for Pedro — one for Diablo ... One for Pedro — one for Diablo ... "

The poor man's eyes popped out like two hard boiled eggs. "*Aaaiii, Dio Mio!*" he gasped, "Saint Peter and the Devil are dividing up the dead souls in the *camposanto!*"

He woke his friend up and the two men sat there staring, their mouths gaping, too frightened to speak. The voice went on: "One for Pedro — one for Diablo ... One for Pedro — one for Diablo ... "

Until finally Pedro and El Diablo got to the bottom of the pile of apples. The two men heard El Diablo's voice say, "Well, Pedro, that's all of them."

But Pedro happened to notice two more apples, right next to the wall. One was a nice, round, fat apple. The other wasn't so good—it was sort of withered up.

They heard Pedro say, "No, Diablo, there are still two more. Don't you see those two right next to the wall—the big fat one and the withered up one?"

The hair stood up on the back of those men's necks! They thought *they* were the ones being talked about. They listened for what would be said next, and they heard El Diablo say, "Well, Pedro, you can take the fat one. I'll take the withered up one."

Then they heard Pedro say, "No, Diablo. Neither one is any good. You can take them both!"

When the two men heard that, they thought the Devil would be coming over the wall any minute to get them. They sobered up in a hurry, jumped to their feet and ran home as fast as they could. They slammed their doors and locked them tight!

And they say that from that day on, those two men stayed home every night. And they never touched another drop of whiskey for the rest of their lives!

Good
Advice

T his is the story of a man and wife who had just one son. He was a good boy, both likeable and hardworking, but sometimes a little slow to learn.

One day the parents told the boy he would have to go look for work and bring some money into the family, as they were very poor.

So the boy set out and soon came to a ranch and began to work there. At the end of the first month, the rancher paid the boy one silver coin, and the boy started for home to give the money to his parents.

On the way, the boy met an old, old man with a long grey beard. *"Buenas tardes,"* the boy greeted him. "What are you doing here on the road?"

The man told him, "I'm selling advice." And he told the boy that for one silver coin he might receive some advice of great value.

So the boy handed the coin to the old man, and the old one whispered in his ear:

> *Dondequiera que fueras,*
> *haz lo que vieras.*
> Wherever you may go,
> do as you see others do.

The boy walked on home repeating that advice over and over to himself. When he got home, and his parents learned that he had spent all his wages on one piece of advice, they scolded him sharply and told him to go back to work.

The boy returned to the ranch and worked another month. He received his silver coin and started for home. Again he met the old man, who said his second bit of advice was even more valuable than the first.

The boy paid him and received these words:

Si eres casado,

que tenga cuidado.

If you're a married man,

be on your guard.

The boy walked on home repeating the rhyme to himself. When he arrived home, his parents were furious. "Foolish boy!" they shouted. "We're depending on you to help us with the money you make, and you waste it on advice. Here's some more advice — go back to work and don't come home until you have some money to offer!"

They chased the boy from the house, and he returned to the ranch. You can guess what happened at the end of the month. Again he met the old man on the road. But this time he hesitated. "If I spend this money, I can't go home," he explained.

"What is money?" asked the old one. "Money comes and it goes. Good advice will last you all your life." And the boy paid his coin to the old man again.

In return, the old man told him:

Aunque pobre, eres sano;

trabaja con la mano.

Although poor, you're a healthy man;

Earn your living with your hands.

With that, the old man disappeared. The boy thought, "Now I can never go home. If I do, they'll chase me off again. I'll go into the world and seek my fortune." And he set out for a foreign land.

After traveling a long time he came to a city built around a great castle. The boy made his way to the castle gate, and there he saw a troop of soldiers marching back and forth with rifles on their shoulders.

Suddenly the boy remembered the first bit of advice he had bought. "I must do what I see being done," he said to himself.

He had no rifle, so he picked up a broom that he saw leaning against a nearby wall and fell in with the soldiers.

Now, it just so happened that the Princess was looking out from her window at that moment, and there is something you must know about her — she was very sad. Indeed, she hadn't laughed in years. She had been sad for so long that her father, the King, had declared that any man who could make her laugh could marry her!

When the Princess saw that boy take up a broom and march along with the soldiers, she burst forth in peals of laughter. The boy was immediately brought into the castle to become the Princess' husband!

But there is something more you must know. The reason for the Princess' sadness was that she had been married a hundred times, but each of her husbands had disappeared on their wedding night, never to be seen again. It was whispered that some horrible monster had eaten them!

Well, the boy was married to the Princess, and after the wedding feast, they went up to her chambers. But the boy remembered the second piece of advice. "I'm a married man now," he told himself. I'd better be careful." And he made up his mind to stay awake all night and be on his guard.

Just at midnight he was beginning to doze off when he heard a slithering and hissing sound. He opened his eyes, and there, not two feet from his face, was the gaping mouth of a great serpent! Its eyes were bright yellow and its long red tongue flashed in and out of its mouth.

The boy jumped up, and seizing a sword that hung on the wall, chopped at the snake until he killed it. That was the monster that had eaten the other bridegrooms — and now it was dead.

In the morning when everyone saw that the Princess' husband was alive, a big celebration was called. It lasted for seven days and seven nights. But the boy kept thinking about the third advice he had bought — although poor you're a healthy man; earn your living with your hands.

"This dancing and feasting is all very nice," the boy told his wife, "but my advice tells me I should be working with my hands." And he declared that the next day he would go find work.

"You're married to a princess," the wife told him. "You don't have to work."

But he insisted. "Your money is yours. I must still earn my own." In the morning he went to the palace of a neighboring king and asked for work. He was put to work building a wall with some other laborers.

The other workmen soon saw that the boy knew nothing about laying stone or mixing mortar, and he struck them as a bit foolish. They all began to make fun of him.

Finally the boy grew angry. "You can say what you like," he told his fellow workers. "But I am married to a princess. Can any of you say as much?"

Of course the other workers didn't believe him. One of them reported to the King that the boy was boasting and pretending to be royalty, claiming that he was married to a princess.

The King was enraged and sent for the boy. But when he saw what a simple fellow he was, the King laughed. "So you claim to be a nobleman."

"No, Your Majesty," the boy replied. "But my wife is a princess."

Now the King laughed louder. But the boy told him, "If you don't believe me wait until noon. You'll see when she brings my lunch."

The King was growing annoyed. "Yes, I'll wait until noon, and if I don't see a princess coming with your lunch, you may expect to spend the rest of your life in my dungeon!"

"Fine," said the boy. "And if you do see a princess, what will you give me?"

"If *you're* married to a princess," the King roared, "I'll pay you your weight in gold!"

The boy went back to work on the wall, and just at twelve o'clock he called to the workers, "Look! Here comes my wife."

Up the road came a carriage drawn by twelve white horses. In front rode fifty mounted soldiers, and fifty more rode behind. The carriage stopped in front of the workmen and the Princess descended.

Now, the King was watching from his window, and when he saw the Princess he began cursing and muttering to himself, but there was no getting out of his bargain.

The boy was weighed, and an equal weight of gold from the King's treasury was measured out. The boy returned home with the Princess, and since they lived happily for the rest of their lives, there's really nothing more to tell about them.

The
Cricket

This is a story about two men who were *compadres*, which means they were godfathers to each other's children.

The one man was rich. He had a fine ranch with a big herd of cattle. And he had one mule that was his pride and joy. It was a prize winning mule.

His *compadre* was very poor. And he was lazy. He never worked, never paid his bills. And he was always talking and talking. The people gave him a nickname. They called him *El Grillo*, The Cricket, because he would never be quiet, just as a cricket won't quiet down when you're trying to get to sleep at night.

One of the foolish things that The Cricket was always saying was that he was *un adivino*, a seer, and that he could solve mysteries and find things that were lost. He used that idea to play a trick on his rich *compadre*.

Whenever The Cricket would get far behind in his bills and owe a lot of money, he would go out to his rich *compadre's* ranch. He would catch that prize winning mule and lead it into the mountains and hide it.

The rich man would look all over his ranch for the mule. Then he would go call on The Cricket. "Can you help me?" he would ask. "My mule is lost. I can't find him anywhere on the ranch. Could you use your powers as a seer and find out where that mule is?"

The Cricket would say, "Oh that doesn't sound too hard. I think I can solve this mystery. But you know, I need some help too. Could you just pay off a few of my bills?"

The rich man would pay The Cricket's bills, and the poor man would go back to the mountains and get the mule and lead it home. Over and over he played the trick on his *compadre*. But his mischief almost caught up with him.

One day the rich man was in Santa Fe visiting the Governor, and the Governor was upset. "Oh," he sighed. "I have lost a ring that I've had since I was a child. I can't find it anywhere in the palace."

The rich man reassured him, "I can help you. My *compadre* is a seer. He can solve mysteries and find things that are lost. I'll tell him to come find your ring."

So the next day The Cricket had to go to the palace to find the ring. Now the pressure was really on him. He would have to find something that was really lost. So he tried to get out of it.

The Governor said, "I understand that you are *un adivino*, that you can find lost articles."

"Oh, no, Your Excellency," The Cricket said. "Sometimes I've been lucky and found something that was lost, but I wouldn't say I'm a seer, or have any special powers."

When he heard that, the Governor became suspicious. He thought, "This man sounds like a fraud to me. He sounds like a cheat."

He told The Cricket, "I'm going to lock you in a

room for three days. If at the end of that time you can tell me where my ring is, you'll get a rich reward. But if you fail, then I'll know you've been lying to the people. And you'll get the proper punishment."

So The Cricket was locked in a room, and of course, he had no idea where the ring was or how he might find out.

Now, the truth of the matter was that three of the kitchen servants had stolen the ring. And it just so happened that on the evening of the first day one of those servants was sent up to The Cricket's room to serve the prisoner his supper.

The servant entered and placed the food on the table, and when The Cricket saw his evening meal before him, a thought hit — he had only three days in which to solve the mystery, and here it was supper-time, the end of the first day!

So as the servant was leaving the room, The Cricket shook his head and muttered to himself, "Ai! Of the three, there goes the first!"

He meant the first of the three days, but when the servant heard him, he thought The Cricket had recognized him as one of the thieves. He ran back to the kitchen. "That man in the room!" he sputtered to his friends. "He really is a seer. As I was leaving the room I heard him say, 'Of the three, there goes the first.' He knew that I was one of the thieves!"

"Don't jump to conclusions," the other two advised. "Tomorrow a different one of us will take his food. We'll see what he says then."

The next day a second servant took the evening

meal to The Cricket's room. Again, when The Cricket saw his supper before him, the truth struck — only three days to save himself, and the second was gone. As the servant was going through the door, The Cricket sighed, "*Ai!* Of the three, there goes the second!"

The servant ran back to his friends. "There can be no doubt about it. He knows! As I was leaving he said, 'Of the three, there goes the second.' He knew that I was one of the thieves too."

So on the third day, when the third servant took The Cricket his food, he just fell on his knees and pleaded, "Please don't tell the Governor. We know that you know about us, but if you tell the Governor, he'll have our heads cut off."

The Cricket realized what the man was talking about. "I won't turn you in," he assured the servant, "if you do exactly as I say. Take the ring out to the barnyard and throw it on the ground in front of the fattest goose in the flock. Make sure the goose swallows the ring."

The servant did as he was told. Later, when the Governor demanded to know where his ring was, The Cricket told him, "Your Excellency, this is very strange, but I had a vision while I was in that room. I saw your barnyard and the pen where the geese are kept. And the ring was in the belly of the fattest goose!"

The Governor laughed, "How would it get there?" But he ordered that the goose be brought in and its stomach opened. There was the ring!

That made a believer of the Governor. He rewarded The Cricket with gold and sent him home with the goose for his wife to cook.

28

After getting out of that one, The Cricket promised himself, "Never again will I call myself a seer." But it wasn't so easy to get out of it.

A few weeks later the Governor of Chihuahua was in New Mexico visiting at the palace, and the Governor of New Mexico just had to brag about The Cricket. "Living here in this province of New Mexico is a man who is *un adivino*," he boasted to the Governor of Chihuahua. "He can solve mysteries and find things that are lost. He could tell you what was hidden in some secret place."

The Governor of Chihuahua laughed, "*Adivino*, indeed! There's no such thing."

The two men started to argue, and before long they made a bet. They bet a thousand dollars apiece.

The arrangement was that the Governor of Chihuahua would hide something in a box, and they would run the box to the top of the flagpole. The Cricket would have to stand on the ground at the bottom of the flagpole and tell what was inside the box.

The day of the contest arrived, and the Governor of Chihuahua got a clever idea. He took a big box and put a smaller box inside it, then a smaller box inside that, and so on, until the last box he put in was very tiny.

"He'll think it's something big in this large box," the Governor laughed. "I'll get something very small to go in this tiny box."

He went out to the garden to look for something small, and just then a little cricket went hopping across the path. The Governor caught it and put it in the smallest box. He sealed all the boxes and raised them to the top of the flagpole. The guards went to get The Cricket.

There the poor Cricket stood at the bottom of the flagpole without a clue what was in the box. But the Governor of New Mexico and the Governor of Chihuahua stood before him, and there were soldiers all around. He couldn't run.

He just stood there. An hour passed, and then another. Finally the Governor of Chihuahua started to laugh. "This man is a fraud, just as I told you." He turned to the Governor of New Mexico. "Pay the bet and let's be done with it."

Now the Governor of New Mexico grew impatient. "Speak up," he told The Cricket. "Tell us what's in the box. Speak!" Finally he roared, "I'll give you one more minute. Speak or I'll have you shot!"

The Cricket had to say something. He stuttered and fumbled, "In the box . . . in the box . . . in the box . . . in the box . . ."

"What?" gasped the Governor of Chihuahua. "How does he know there's a box inside a box inside a box!"

And just then, thinking of himself, The Cricket hung his head and cried, "Oh no! They've got you this time, you poor little Cricket!"

The Governor of Chihuahua's jaw fell. "If I hadn't heard that with my own ears, I never would have believed it!" He drew out his wallet and paid a thousand dollars to the Governor of New Mexico.

The Governor of New Mexico gave five hundred of those dollars to The Cricket. He shook his hand and slapped him on the back. "Well done again!" And he sent him home.

That was too close a call for The Cricket. "Never, ever again in my whole life will I tell anyone I have any special powers whatever!"

But the boys on his street had always liked to make fun of The Cricket. That day they had filled a big gunny sack with garbage, and as The Cricket started down the street they ran out to meet him.

They waved the gunny sack in front of him. "*Adivino*," they taunted, "use your secret powers. Tell us what's inside this gunny sack."

"Don't call me *adivino*,"The Cricket snapped. "I don't believe in that any more. It's nothing but a bunch of garbage. Leave me alone!"

The boys stared at him in amazement. "How did he know it was garbage? He really is a seer! We thought he was just an old fool."

So from that day on, no matter how hard The Cricket tried to tell people, "No! I'm not a seer. I have no special powers at all," they wouldn't believe him. Every time a housewife lost a spoon, she would come to him to find it. The Governor kept calling him to solve mysteries.

Finally, in order to have any peace at all, he had to take his family, and move far away from New Mexico, to a place where they hadn't heard of men who are called *adivinos*, or seers. And if he hasn't died, he must still be living there.

La Hormiguita
▬▬ (The Little Ant) ▬▬

All through the long, cold winter La Hormiguita, the little ant, had to stay inside her underground home because the ground was all covered with snow. But now the snow was melted, so she went to the door with her mother to see if spring had come.

"Look, Mamá," she said, "the snow has melted. And the grass is turning green. It's springtime! May I go outside and play?"

"No, *Mi 'jita*," her mother said. "Don't you see those dark clouds? And can't you feel how cold it is? It may still snow. You'd better stay inside."

But La Hormiguita didn't do as she was told. When her mother was busy, she ran outside to play. She climbed to the very tip of each green blade of grass she came to. She ran upside down on low branches of bushes and trees. She went a long way from home.

But pretty soon La Hormiguita began to feel cold. "Mamá was right," she thought. "I'm going back inside."

But just as she started for home, big, papery flakes of snow began to float down from the sky. And one big snowflake landed right on La Hormiguita's little leg and stuck it fast to the ground.

La Hormiguita tugged and tugged at her little leg. And she cried out to *La Nieve*, the snow, to let go of it so she could go home. She said:

> Nieve, suelta mi patita
> pá que vaya a mi casita!

But the snow wouldn't let go of her little leg. So La Hormiguita called out to *El Sol*, the sun, to melt the snow:

> Sol, derrite Nieve.
> Nieve, suelta mi patita
> pá que vaya a mi casita!

But the sun wouldn't melt the snow. So La Hormiguita called out to *La Nube*, the cloud, to cover the sun:

> Nube, tapa Sol.
> Sol, derrite Nieve.
> Nieve, suelta mi patita
> pá que vaya a mi casita!

But the cloud wouldn't cover the sun. So La Hormiguita called out to *El Viento*, the wind, to scatter the cloud:

> Viento, desbarata Nube.
> Nube, tapa Sol.
> Sol, derrite Nieve.
> Nieve, suelta mi patita
> pá que vaya a mi casita!

But the wind wouldn't scatter the cloud. So La Hormiguita called out to *La Pared*, the wall, to block the wind:

> Pared, ataja Viento.
> Viento, desbarata Nube.
> Nube, tapa Sol.
> Sol, derrite Nieve.
> Nieve, suelta mi patita
> pá que vaya a mi casita!

But the wall wouldn't block the wind. So La Hormiguita called out to *El Ratón*, the mouse to gnaw holes in the wall:

> *Ratón, agujerea Pared.*
> *Pared, ataja Viento.*
> *Viento, desbarata Nube.*
> *Nube, tapa Sol.*
> *Sol, derrite Nieve.*
> *Nieve, suelta mi patita*
> *pá que vaya a mi casita!*

But the mouse wouldn't gnaw holes in the wall. So La Hormiguita called out to *El Gato*, the cat, to catch the mouse:

> *Gato, coge Ratón.*
> *Ratón agujerea Pared.*
> *Pared, ataja Viento.*
> *Viento, desbarata Nube.*
> *Nube, tapa Sol.*
> *Sol, derrite Nieve.*
> *Nieve, suelta mi patita*
> *pá que vaya a mi casita!*

But the cat wouldn't catch the mouse. So La Hormiguita called out to *El Perro*, the dog, to chase the cat:

> *Perro, persigue Gato.*
> *Gato, coge Ratón.*
> *Ratón agujerea Pared.*
> *Pared, ataja Viento.*
> *Viento, desbarata Nube.*
> *Nube, tapa Sol.*
> *Sol, derrite Nieve.*
> *Nieve, suelta mi patita*
> *pá que vaya a mi casita!*

But do you think the dog would chase the cat? No! He wouldn't do it. So La Hormiguita called out to *La Pulga*, the little flea that lives on the dog, to bite the dog:

> *Pulga, pica Perro.*
> *Perro, persigue Gato.*
> *Gato, coge Ratón.*
> *Ratón, agujerea Pared.*
> *Pared, ataja Viento.*
> *Viento, desbarata Nube.*
> *Nube, tapa Sol.*
> *Sol, derrite Nieve.*
> *NIEVE, SUELTA MI PATITA*
> *PÁ QUE VAYA A MI CASITA!*

Well! The flea is a cousin to the ant. And when she heard La Hormiguita crying out for help:

> The flea began to bite the dog.
> The dog began to chase the cat.
> The cat began to catch the mouse.
> The mouse began to gnaw the wall.
> The wall began to block the wind.
> The wind began to scatter the cloud.
> The cloud began to block the sun.
> The sun began to melt the snow...

The snow let go of La Hormiguita's little leg. And she finally made it back home safely.

And she waited until her mother said that *spring had come for sure* before she went back outside to play.

The Best
Thief

L ong ago there lived a poor man and his wife who had three sons. But they didn't have any money to feed and clothe the boys.

Now, in those days people were very helpful to one another. If a family was too poor to raise a child, the godparents, the *padrinos*, would take the child and raise it as their own.

So the man spoke to his *compadres*, the boys' godfathers, and asked them to raise the boys. He also asked that they teach the boys whatever trade they followed, so that the boys could earn a living when they were grown.

The oldest son's godfather was a cobbler, so the boy lived with him and learned to cut and stitch leather into shoes. The boy could soon make better shoes than his godfather, so he went home to live with his parents and help them out by working at his trade.

The second son's godfather was a tailor, and the boy learned how to measure and cut cloth and sew fine clothes. When he had become a better tailor than his godfather, he returned home.

Now, the godfather of the youngest boy — he was a thief! People said he was *El Mejor Ladron*, the best thief in the land. From him the boy learned how to steal things.

One day the thief told the boy, "Come. Let's walk down the road together until I find a way to test you to see if you're clever enough to be a thief."

They walked along until they came to a tree by the side of the road. Up in the tree was a bird's nest with the mother bird sitting on her eggs.

The thief said, "I'm going to climb this tree and steal the eggs from under that mother bird. She won't feel a thing. I won't make her fly away.

"I'll bring them to you. If you can climb back up the tree and put the eggs back under the mother without scaring her off, then I'll know that you're good enough to be a thief."

So the thief climbed the tree. But without his knowing it, the boy climbed the tree right behind him.

The thief stole the first egg from under the mother bird and put it in his pocket, and the boy stole the egg from the man's pocket and put it in his own. Then the thief stole a second egg, and the boy stole that one. And the same with the third.

Then the two of them climbed down without the thief's ever knowing that the boy was right there below him.

When they got to the ground, the man said, "Now it's your turn. Take these eggs . . . " He reached into his pocket but there weren't any eggs.

The boy reached into his own pocket. "Oh," he said, "do you mean these eggs?" There were the three eggs in the boy's hand.

The man laughed. "They used to say that I was the best thief in the land. But I guess I'm second best.

You're the best thief in the land!" And he sent the boy home to his parents so that he could help them out by working at his trade.

Now back in those times the only place to find a job was at the King's palace. The oldest son had gone there as soon as he returned home and because of his skill had become the Royal Cobbler.

When the second son returned, he also found work at the palace, and soon he was the Royal Tailor.

When the youngest son arrived home, the two older brothers went to speak to the King, hoping that the boy might also be able to find work at the palace.

"Well," asked the King, "what sort of work does he do?"

"He's a thief, Your Majesty. He's the best thief in the whole land!"

"A thief!" the King roared. "I usually hang thieves. I don't give them a job! But you say he's the best thief in the whole land? I'm curious about that. Tell him to come and talk to me tomorrow."

The next day the boy went to speak with the King. The King said, "I hear that you're the best thief in the land."

"Well then, Your Majesty," the boy said, "you've heard the truth."

"We'll see about that. I'm going to give you a test. Tomorrow a pack train of mules loaded with gold will be coming to the palace. If you can steal the gold from those mules without the mule drivers catching you, it's yours. But if they catch you, you'll spend thirty years in my dungeon!"

The boy just shrugged his shoulders and went away. He went to talk to his brother the cobbler, and he had his brother take leather and make a big doll. The doll was as big as a full-grown man. The boy set out down the road with the doll over his shoulder.

The boy came to a grove of cottonwood trees not far from the road. He climbed one of those trees with the doll and set it up among the branches. Then he went off to hide.

A short while later the mule train came up the road. The mule drivers looked over at the tree. They could see someone hiding among the branches.

"Mira, son los apaches! It's the Apaches!" some said. Others said, "No. *Son los navajoses.* It's the Navajos."

But they all knew that whether it was the Apaches or the Navajos, the smart thing was to go right on by and pretend they hadn't seen that Indian scout watching them.

That night when they made camp, they were nervous. They put out double guards and they all slept with their rifles next to them in their bed rolls.

The boy waited until late into the night. Then he came running into the camp screaming, *"Los apaches! Los apaches!* Here come the Apaches!"

The mule drivers jumped up and grabbed their rifles. They all ran for the trees, to fight from behind them.

While the mule drivers were gone, the boy opened all the saddle bags, took the gold, closed the saddle bags again and went on his way.

When the boy arrived at the palace the next day, the King was furious. "So!" he bellowed, "you got my gold!"

"Your Majesty," the boy corrected, "you mean *my* gold, don't you?"

"Aaahh, your gold or my gold — whatever! Now I

40

have another test. Tomorrow another pack train will be coming, and these drivers will be wise to you. If you can get their gold, fine, it's yours. But if you fail, you've taken your last look at sunlight. You'll spend the rest of your life in my dungeon."

The boy shrugged and went off to see his brother the tailor. He had him take black cloth and make eleven black robes such as priests wear.

He wrapped those robes up in a bundle and set out. He only made one stop on his way, and that was to buy a big jug of whiskey.

That evening the mule drivers were coming up the road and they met up with a priest coming down the road from the other direction. He was all covered with dust from his journey, and he carried a bundle under his arm.

They greeted him courteously. "Father," they said, "will you stop and camp the night with us?"

"No," the priest replied, "I have to get on to the next village. The people are expecting me. But I would appreciate a cup of coffee. Could you give me that?"

"Of course, Father. It's time to make camp anyway." So they built a campfire and put on a big coffee pot. Then the men got busy with their animals, giving them water and hay.

While they were busy, the boy—because that's who the priest really was—took the lid from the coffee pot, pulled the stopper from the jug of whiskey and poured the whole jug of whiskey into the coffee pot.

When the men finished their work, they poured

out cups of coffee. The boy only pretended to drink his. He poured it out on the ground.

But the men drained that first cup of coffee. "Whew! That's good coffee. Let's have another cup!" They poured out another round. "Ah! That coffee gets better with every cup. Let's have some more!"

Soon they were all swaying back and forth and singing around the fire. Then they fell asleep. While they were sleeping, the boy not only stole the gold — he also stole their clothes. And he dressed them all up like priests in black robes.

The next day the watchman at the palace was looking out and he saw ten priests come walking up the road. "What's this?" he puzzled. "Oh! The Bishop must be coming for a visit!" He ran to inform the priest at the palace.

They started ringing the church bell, and everyone turned out. Even the King and Queen were waiting in their royal finery — to meet their own mule drivers dressed up like priests!

When the boy got to the palace, the King was fuming. "Sooo! you got my gold again, did you?"

"Your Majesty! You mean *my* gold, don't you?"

"Your gold! My gold!" the King thundered. "Who cares? I have one more test for you. And this time you won't succeed!"

"Maybe I will. Maybe I won't."

"You won't! Listen to this! Can you come into my bedroom tonight and steal the sheets from my bed while the Queen and I are sleeping on it? Ha! Ha! If you can do that I'll give you half my kingdom! But if you fail — and you *will* fail — it will cost you your life!"

The boy thought about it for awhile. Then he went back to that big cottonwood tree where he had left the doll. He got the doll down and went along to his own home.

His father had just butchered a sheep, so he cut the doll open and stuffed the insides of that sheep into the doll. He sewed it back up and went on to the palace to await nightfall.

That night the King was lying in bed with his eyes wide open, staring at the door, just waiting for someone to try to come in. He had his sharpest sword at his side.

The boy waited until far into the night. Then he held the doll in front of him and went creeping up the stairs to the royal bed chamber. When he got to the doorway, he eased that doll ahead of him into the room.

The King saw someone coming through the door and leaped out of bed. He seized his sword and — slash! The doll fell in two pieces. And blood from the insides of the sheep went splattering all over the room.

"Aha!" the King laughed. "I guess I'm rid of that thief at last." But then he thought, "I can't leave this dead body here for the Queen to see in the morning. I'd better bury him."

So he picked up the two halves of that doll, which he thought was the thief, and carried it out to bury it.

While he was gone, the boy came sneaking into the room. And he climbed into bed with the Queen!

"Whew!" he said, "I'm so hot and sweaty! It was a

lot of work burying that thief. He was heavy! Move over to the far side of the bed and give me plenty of air."

So the Queen moved over as far as she could on the bed. And the boy slipped the sheets off half the bed. Then he said, "I'm still too warm. Let me get close to the window. You come over here!"

So the Queen traded places with him, and he took the sheets off the other half of the bed. Then, as soon as the Queen drifted back to sleep, he crept from the room.

He had hardly gone out the door, when the King came in. The King climbed into bed, and *he* said, "Whew! I'm so hot and sweaty! It was a lot of work burying that thief. He was heavy!"

The Queen opened one eye. "You already said that once!" she scolded. "Are you going to talk about it all night? Can't I get some sleep?"

"What do you mean—'Already said that once. Talk about it all night long'? What are you...?" Then he noticed that there weren't any sheets on the bed!

He jumped out of bed and started tearing his hair and cursing and kicking the furniture around the room! But what could he do? He had given his word. And so the next day he had to sign a piece of paper giving half his kingdom to the boy.

The boy took his father and mother and his two brothers, and they all moved into one of the small palaces on their half of the kingdom.

And from that day on the family was so rich, no one in the family ever had to work again. Not as a cobbler. Not as a tailor. And not even as a thief!

Little Gold
Star

A long time ago there was a man whose wife had died. He had just one daughter, and her name was Arcía. Their neighbor was a woman whose husband had died. And she had two daughters.

Every day, when Arcía walked down the street past the woman's house, the woman came out and gave her something good to eat. She gave her sweet little cookies called *biscochitos*, or *sopaipillas* with honey— sometimes some milk to drink.

And so one day Arcía said to her father, "Papá, why don't you marry that woman? She's so good to me! She gives me *sopaipillas* almost every day."

Her father didn't want to. He said:

No, Mi 'jita . . .
Si hoy nos da sopaipillas con miel,
mañana nos dará sopaipillas con hiel!

No, Daughter . . .

If she gives us sopaipillas with honey today, tomorrow she'll give us sopaipillas with gall!

But Arcía protested, "No, Papá. She's a nice woman. You should marry her." And she talked her father into it!

For a while everything was fine. But before long the girls started quarreling among themselves, and the woman no longer liked Arcía and began to be very unkind to her.

45

She bought all sorts of fine things for her own daughters — pretty dresses and jewels for them to wear. But when Arcía's shoes wore out, she wouldn't even buy her new ones. And Arcía had to go around barefoot.

Finally the bedroom was so full of the beautiful things that belonged to the step sisters, there wasn't room for Arcía to sleep there. She had to move down to the kitchen and sleep next to the stove.

This went on for some time. And then one day the man went to his ranch in the mountains, and when he returned, he brought with him three young sheep. He gave one sheep to each girl.

"Tend your sheep carefully," he told each girl. "When it is full grown you can sell it and keep the money. Or, if you prefer, I'll butcher it, and the family can eat the meat — whichever you wish."

So the girls began raising their sheep. Arcía took the best care of hers. Before long, it was the fattest of the three.

One day she told her father, "Papá, I want you to kill my sheep and butcher it. I'm going to roast it and invite the whole village for a big supper."

So her father took the sheep and killed it. Now, back in those days, people were very poor. They couldn't afford to waste any part of an animal they had killed. They would even use the intestines — the *tripitas* they called them.

So when the man had cleaned out the sheep, he told Arcía to take the *tripitas* down to the river to wash them.

Well, for a child nowadays, that would be a very unpleasant task. But in those times they thought nothing of it. Arcía picked up the insides of her sheep and went down to the river to wash them off.

Suddenly, a big hawk swooped down out of the sky and snatched the *tripitas* from her hand. Arcía called out to the hawk, "*Señor Gavilán*, bring those things back to me, please."

The hawk called down to her: "Look . . . where . . . I . . . flyyyyy . . . ."

So she did. She looked up to see where the bird had gone. And when she looked up, down from the sky came a little gold star, and it fastened itself right on her forehead.

She went running home, and when her step sisters saw her, they were jealous. "Oh!" they whispered, "why shouldn't we have a gold star on our foreheads too?" So they went looking for their step father to have him butcher their sheep.

The first one found him and ordered him to kill

her sheep. She went down to the river with the insides and began to wash them off. For a second time the hawk swooped down and snatched them away.

"*Gavilán malvado!*" she screamed. "You rotten bird, bring those things back to me!"

"Look . . . where . . . I . . . flyyyyy . . . ."

"Don't tell me where to look. I'll look wherever I please. Bring back my things this minute."

But finally she did have to look up to see where the hawk had gone. When she looked up, down from the sky came a long, floppy donkey ear, and it fastened itself to her forehead!

She ran home crying, and her mother gasped, "Bring me the scissors!" She took the scissors and snipped off the donkey ear. But a longer and floppier one grew in its place.

From that day on, everyone in the village called out *Oreja de Burro!* whenever the girl walked by. And that became her name — Donkey Ear!

But her sister hadn't heard what happened, and she was already on her way to the river with the *tripitas* from her sheep. She knelt down to wash them, and the hawk snatched then away.

"You good-for-nothing bird! Bring those back."

"Look . . . where . . . I . . . flyyyyy . . . ."

"I don't have to obey you. Bring back my things this instant!"

But she too had to look up to see where the hawk had gone. When she looked up, down from the sky came a long, green cow horn, fastening itself on her forehead.

Her mother cried, "Bring me the saw!" She tried to saw the horn off, but the more she cut, the longer and greener it grew.

From that day on, everyone called that girl *Cuerno Verde* — Green Horn!

Now, it just so happened that right about this time the Prince of that land decided that he would like to get married. But he couldn't think of a single girl living in his village who he might fall in love with.

Then he got an idea. He decided to give a big party and invite the girls from all the villages throughout the mountains, so that he could find one to be his bride.

The day of the party arrived, and Arcía helped her step sisters get dressed in their fine gowns. She fixed their hair and tried to cover those strange things on their foreheads. Then she waved goodbye as they went off to the party. Arcía didn't even have a pair of shoes, let alone a pretty party dress, so she had to stay home.

But that night, all by herself at home, she began to feel lonely. She thought, "It won't do any harm if I just go to the palace and peek in the window and see what a grand party is like."

So she went to the palace and crept up to the window and peeked in. When she peeked in through the window, the gold star on her forehead started to shine more brightly than the sun! It caught everyone's attention.

The Prince said, "Have that girl with the gold star come in here!" And his servants ran to get Arcía.

But when Arcía saw the servants coming, she
was frightened, and she ran home as fast as she could.
The next day, the Prince and his servants started
going from house to house, looking for the girl with
the gold star. They arrived at Arcía's house, but her

step mother made her hide under the trough in the kitchen, and wouldn't even let her come out.

The woman introduced her own daughters: "Your Majesty, perhaps these are the girls you are looking for. Aren't they lovely young women?"

The Prince looked at the girls and saw the donkey ear and the cow horn on their foreheads. "No! I don't think those were the girls I had in mind." He started backing toward the door.

But just as he reached the door, the cat came up and rubbed against his ankle. The cat said, *"Ñaaauuu, ñaaauuu. Arcía debajo de la artesa está?"*

What?" demanded the Prince. "Did the cat say someone is under the trough?"

"No," laughed the woman. "The cat's just hungry." She picked it up and threw it outside.

But the cat came back and rubbed against his other ankle. *"Ñaaauuu. Arcía debajo de la artesa está."*

The Prince insisted, "The cat says someone is under the trough. Who is it?" And he sent his servants to find out.

When Arcía saw the servants approach, she stood up. When she stood up, her ugly, dirty old clothes turned into a beautiful gown. The Prince fell in love with her immediately and asked her to marry him.

Arcía said she would. And a few days later the wedding celebration began. It lasted for nine days and nine nights—and the last day was better than the first. And everyone was invited—even the mean old step mother and her two daughters: *Cuerno Verde* and *Oreja de Burro*.

La Llorona
■ (The Crying Woman) ■

H ere is the best known story in the Southwest. And it is known all over Mexico as well. There are many ways of telling the story and wherever you here it, the teller will swear that it happened in that very town. In Santa Fe you might hear it like this:

The story began long ago, when the city we call Santa Fe was a little village called *La Villa Real de la Santa Fé de San Francisco de Asís*. That was a long name for a tiny village. And living in that village was one girl who was far prettier than any other. Her name was María.

People said María was certainly the prettiest girl in New Mexico. She might even be the most beautiful girl in the world. But because María was so beautiful, she thought she was better than everyone else.

María came from a hard-working family, and they had one of the finest homes in Santa Fe. They provided her with pretty clothes to wear. But she was never satisfied. She thought she deserved far better things.

When María became a young woman, she would have nothing to do with the youths from Santa Fe and the nearby villages. She was too good for them.

Often as she was walking with her grandmother through the countryside surrounding Santa Fe, she would say to her grandmother, *"Abuelita,* when I get married, I'll marry the most handsome man in

New Mexico."

The grandmother would just shake her head. But María would look out across the hillside and go on, "His hair will be as black and shiny as the raven I see sitting on that piñon tree. And when he moves, he will be as strong and graceful as the stallion *Abuelito* has in his corral."

"María," the old woman would sigh, "why are you always talking about what a man looks like? If you're going to marry a man, just be sure that he's a good man. Be sure he has a good heart in him. Don't worry so much about his face."

But María would say to herself, "These old people! They have such foolish old ideas. They don't understand."

Well, one day a man came to Santa Fe who seemed to be just the man María was talking about. His name was Gregorio. He was a cowboy from the *llano* east of the mountains.

He could ride anything. In fact, if he was riding a horse and it got well trained, he would give it away and go rope a wild horse. He thought it wasn't manly for him to ride a horse that wasn't half wild.

He was so handsome that all the girls were falling in love with him. He could play the guitar and sing beautifully. María made up her mind. That was the man she would marry.

But she didn't let on. If they passed on the street and Gregorio greeted her, she would look away. He came to her house and played his guitar and sang. She wouldn't even come to the window.

Before long, Gregorio made up *his* mind. "That haughty, proud girl María," he told himself. "That's the girl I'll marry. I can win her heart!" So things turned out just as María had planned.

María's parents didn't like the idea of her marrying Gregorio. "He won't make a good husband," they told her. "He's used to the wild life of the plains. He'll be gone on buffalo hunts and cattle drives, or drinking wine with his friends. Don't marry him."

Of course, María wouldn't listen to her parents. She married Gregorio. And for a time things were fine. They had two children.

But after a few years, Gregorio went back to his old ways. He would be gone for months at a time.

When he returned, he would say to María, "I didn't come to see you. I just want to visit my children for a while." He would play with the children, and go off to the cantina to drink wine and gamble all night long. And he began to court other women.

As proud as María was, she became very jealous of those other women. And she began to feel jealous of her own children as well, because Gregorio paid attention to them, but ignored her.

One evening, María was standing out in front of her house with her two children beside her when Gregorio came riding by in a hired carriage. Another woman sat on the seat beside him. He stopped and spoke to his children, but didn't even look at María. He just drove up the street.

At the sight of that, something just seemed to burst inside María. She felt such anger and jealousy!

And it all turned against her children.

She seized her two children by the arm and dragged them along with her to the river. And she threw her own children into the water.

But as they disappeared with the current, María realized what she had done. She ran along the bank of the river, reaching out her arms, as though she might snatch her children back from the current. But they were long gone.

She ran on, driven by the anger and guilt that filled her heart. She wasn't paying attention to where she was going, and her foot caught on a root. She tripped and fell forward. Her forehead struck a rock. And she was killed.

The next day her parents looked all over town for her. Then someone brought the word that her body lay out on the bank of the river.

They brought her body back into Santa Fe, but

because of what she'd done, the priest wouldn't let her be buried in the *camposanto*, the holy graveyard. "Take her out and bury her on the bank of the river!" he commanded.

So her parents buried her there on the river bank where she had been found. And many people in Santa Fe say they know exactly where she was buried, because a big building stands there today. It's called the New Mexico State Capitol!

But they also tell that the first night she was in the grave, she wouldn't rest at peace. She was up and walking along the bank of the river. They saw her moving through the trees, dressed in a long, winding white sheet, as a corpse is dressed for burial.

And they heard her crying through the night. Sometimes they thought it was the wind. But at other times they were sure they could hear the words she was saying: *"Aaaaaiiii...mis hijos...Donde están mis hijos...?"*

"Where are my children?" she cried. She went all up and down the banks of the river, through all the arroyos to the base of the mountains and back down.

Night after night they saw her and heard her. Before long, no one spoke of her as María any longer. They called her by a name every boy and girl in New Mexico knows—*La Llorona*, the weeping woman.

And they told the children, "When it gets dark, you get home! *La Llorona* is out looking for her children. She's so crazy, if she sees you, she won't know if it's you or her own child. She'll pick you up and carry you away! We'll never see you again."

The children heed that warning. They may play

56

along the rivers and arroyos during the daytime, but when the sun sets, they hurry home!

II

Many tales are told of children who narrowly escaped being caught by *La Llorona*. One is about a boy who didn't believe she existed.

"Do you believe that nonsense?" he would ask his friends. "That's just a story parents made up to frighten children."

One evening the boys were playing out on the bank of the river and it began to grow late. "It's getting dark," the other boys said. "We'd better get home."

But not that one boy. "No," he said. "I'm having fun. I'll stay out here a while longer."

The other boys couldn't believe what they were hearing. "Aren't you afraid of *La Llorona*?"

"*La Llorona!*" he laughed. "There's no such thing."

The other boys went home and left that one boy by himself. He had a good time throwing sticks into the river and hitting them with rocks as they floated past. It grew dark. The moon rose.

Suddenly, the boy felt cold all over, as though an icy wind were blowing through his clothes. And all around him there were dogs barking. He looked around and saw a white shape coming toward him through the trees.

He tried to run, but somehow his legs had no strength in them. He couldn't move. He sat there trembling as the shape drew nearer. And he could hear the high, wailing voice, "*Aaaaiiii...mis hijoooos...*"

57

Still he couldn't move. He crouched low, hoping she wouldn't see him. But suddenly she stopped. "*Mi 'jo!*" she cried, "my little boy!" And she came toward him.

His face was as white as the sheet that *La Llorona* was wearing! But still he couldn't run. She approached him and reached out her long fingers and took hold of his shoulders. When *La Llorona's* fingers touched his shoulders, it felt like icicles were cutting into the flesh!

Just then, when *La Llorona* was about to pick him up and carry him away, back in Santa Fe the Cathedral bell started ringing, calling the people to Mass. When the church bell started to ring, *La Llorona* looked over her shoulder furtively, dropped the boy, and disappeared into the trees.

The boy sat there for a long time, gathering his strength and courage together. Finally he was able to run home.

When he got home, his mother was furious. "Where have you been?" she demanded. "You should have been home hours ago!"

The boy stuttered and stammered, *"M-M-Mamá ...La Llorona!"*

"Nonsense! Don't go making up stories about *La Llorona*. You should have been home a long time ago." She reached out to grab him. She was going to give him a good shaking.

But when she reached out to take hold of his shoulders, she noticed that on each shoulder there were five round, red marks — like five blood stains. They had been left by *La Llorona's* fingers!

Then she believed him. She took that shirt and washed it over and over. She tried every trick she knew. But she could never remove those stains.

She carried that shirt all around the neighborhood and showed it to the children. "Look here," she said. "You count these — one ... two ... three ... four ... five! Those stains were left by *La Llorona's* fingers. *La Llorona can* carry children away. When it gets dark, you get home!"

And you can be sure that the children in that neighborhood got home when it got dark. But no one seems to know what became of the shirt, so who can say if the story is true?

Juan
▬▬▬ Camisón ▬▬▬

There was once a poor woman who had a lazy son. The hardest thing he did each day was to decide whether to stay in bed late or get up early so that he'd have more time to lie around and do nothing.

On winter mornings the old woman would wake up cold and call to her son to get up and see if the fire was still burning: *"Juanito, levántate, por favor. Mira ver si hay lumbre."*

Lazy Juan would call the cat, "Pssst, psst." And when he felt that the cat's side was warm, he'd know that the fire was still burning. *Sí, Mamá,"* he would yawn. *"Sí, hay lumbre."* And he'd roll over and go back to sleep.

On summer mornings, the poor woman's first thought was of her garden where she raised what little food they had to eat. As soon as she awoke she'd ask her son to go see if it had rained during the night. *"Juanito, mira ver si cayó agua."*

But Juan wouldn't get up. He would just whistle for the dog and feel its fur. When he felt that the fur was wet: *"Sí, Mamá, cayó agua."*

So you see how lazy Juan was. But in spite of that, and even though there was little in the house to eat, he grew to be a very large boy. He grew so large, in fact, that his mother couldn't afford to buy him proper clothes. She dressed him in a long shirt that hung to his knees, and that was all he wore.

Because of his strange clothes, people started calling him Juan Camisón — Big Shirt Juan. Whenever he walked out the children would dance along behind him chanting:

Juan Camisón, te falta pantalón!

Juan Camisón, you've got no pants on!

Finally Juan got so big that his mother couldn't feed him any longer, and she sent him out into the world to earn his own living.

Juan started down the road, and when he had been walking for about an hour, he saw an old sombrero that someone had thrown away by the side of the road. Juan picked up the hat and put it on his head, thinking he looked quite fine in it.

A short way farther down the road Juan saw a spring by the side of the road and thought he'd get a drink. But when he stooped down to drink, he saw several flies in the mud by the water's edge.

"Ho!" said Juan. "I'm not going to share my water with flies." And he took off his hat and swatted those flies.

What a good hit! Juan counted the flies he had killed and there were seven of them! He felt very proud of himself and wanted the world to know how great he was. So he took some of the mud and wrote on his sombrero:

Soy Juan Camisón
que mata a siete de un empujón!
I'm Juan Camisón
who kills seven at a blow!

And after all that work, Juan was tired and decided to take a nap. He leaned against a tree, and pulled his sombrero down over his face and went to sleep.

While he was asleep, the King's messenger happened to come riding by. He saw Juan sleeping against a tree and thought that he had never seen such a big man. Then he read the words on Juan's sombrero. "What's this?" he said to himself. "A man who kills seven with one blow! That's just the sort of man I'm looking for."

For you must know that the King was fighting a bitter war with an enemy king, and his only hope of victory had rested on a strong man named Macario. But the enemy had found a way to poison Macario's food, and the champion died. The King had sent his messenger to search for a new hero—and here was a man who killed seven with one blow!

The messenger galloped back to tell the King of his find. The King himself rode out to ask Juan Camisón to be his new champion. Before Juan knew what was happening he found himself with the King's army at the battlefield being dressed for combat.

The General sent for a suit of armor for Juan, but the only armor big enough to fit him was that of the dead hero Macario. And the only horse strong enough to carry Juan was Macario's own charger.

So Juan Camisón was dressed in Macario's armor and hoisted into the saddle. Poor Juan Camisón! He had never ridden a horse before. He swayed back and forth in the saddle and clung to the horse's mane with both hands.

And that horse was so fierce and battle-crazy that when he saw the enemy army, he reared up and then charged at full gallop.

Juan bounced up and down in the saddle, flopping from one side of the horse to the other. All the while he was screaming to his companions that he was falling. "*Me caigo yo! Me caigo yo!*"

"I'm falling! I'm falling!" he continued to scream as the horse raced across the battlefield toward the enemy. Juan's arms and legs thrashed wildly in the air.

When the enemy saw him, they couldn't believe their eyes. They thought they had killed Macario, but here was this wild man charging furiously toward them with horse and armor they recognized as Macario's. When he drew nearer, they could hear his screams. "*Me caigo yo! Me caigo yo!*"

To them it sounded as though he was shouting, "Macario! Macario!"

"Do you hear that?" they said to one to the other. "He's saying 'Macario! Macario!' Macario has returned from the dead. He wants us to know he's coming for revenge! Who can fight a man who overcomes death itself?"

They started to retreat. And just then Juan's horse took him past a small tree. Juan reached out and grabbed the trunk to pull himself from the saddle, but the tree had shallow roots and came out of the ground in his hands. He charged on flailing the tree madly about his head.

"Look!" cried the enemy soldiers. "He's pulling

the very trees up by the roots. Run for your lives!"
And they all turned and fled.

When the enemy king got word of what had happened on the battlefield, he sent messages of peace immediately and returned to his own country.

Juan Camisón was presented to his own king and richly rewarded with gold. He took all his money home to his old mother and she danced up and down in her joy.

But as for Juan Camisón—he went back to bed, and he's probably sleeping there still.

The
Prince

There is an old story about a young man whose
father was a king, and whose mother was a queen.
Of course, that would make him a prince.

Then his father and his mother died — so he
should have become king. But in his land they had a
law which said you had to be married to be the king.
He didn't have a wife.

But the Prince heard about a king in a faraway
country who had a beautiful daughter, so he thought
he would go there and see if she would marry him. He
loaded four mules with gold, and started on his long
journey.

He had been traveling for three days, when he
came to a clearing in the forest. He saw a big man
working with an ax, cutting firewood. The man had
made thirty big stacks of firewood. But the Prince
looked all around, and he didn't see any animals — no
oxen or mules or burros — to take the firewood home.

The Prince went up to the man and said, "How
are you going to get this firewood home?"

The man looked puzzled. "Get it home?" he
asked. "I'll carry it home."

The Prince was amazed. "You can carry thirty
stacks of firewood?"

"Of course I can. My name is Cargín-Cargón. I
can carry anything." He picked up the thirty stacks of

66

firewood and carried them home on his shoulders.

When the Prince saw how strong the man was, he asked him to work as a servant and offered to pay him with gold. So Cargín-Cargón became a servant of the Prince, and they traveled along together.

Three days later, they came to a mountain. Sitting at the foot of the mountain was a young man. But as they watched, the young man jumped up and ran off in one direction. They had hardly blinked their eyes, when he came back from the other direction!

They went up to him and said, "Did you really do what it looked like you did? Did you run clear around that mountain in the blink of an eye?"

The man shrugged. "Of course I did. My name is Corrín-Corrón. I can run faster than that when I want to."

So the Prince hired him to be his servant also. And they traveled along together — the Prince, Cargín-Cargón and Corrín-Corrón.

Three days later they saw a man with a rifle, taking careful aim. But when they looked about they couldn't see the animal he was going to shoot. They walked up to him and asked, "What are you going to shoot?"

He told them, "There's a fly sitting on a tree about two miles away. I'm going to shoot his left eye out!"

"You can shoot that well?"

Of course I can. My name is Tirín-Tirón. I never miss anything I shoot at."

The Prince hired him to be his servant. They all

traveled together—the Prince, Cargín-Cargón, Corrín-Corrón, and Tirín-Tirón.

Three days later they saw a man lying with his ear against the ground listening. They stepped up quietly and whispered, "What are you listening for?"

He hushed them. "Shhh. Over in China, a woman dropped a needle on the ground. I'm listening to it bounce."

"You can hear a needle drop on the other side of the world?"

Of course. My name is Escuchín-Escuchón. I hear everything in this world and the other world too."

The Prince hired him to be his servant, and they all traveled along together—the Prince, Cargín-Cargón, Corrín-Corrón, Tirín-Tirón, and Escuchín-Escuchón!

Three days later they came to the faraway kingdom. But they found out that the King was very jealous and didn't want any man to marry his daughter. If a man came there wanting to marry her, he would have to pass some very difficult tests.

First, he would have to run a race with the Princess. She was a fast runner. And if he lost the race, the King would cut off his feet. Already two hundred young men had lost their feet!

But the Prince went to the King and said, "I'm not worried at all about the race. It will be so easy, I'll just let my servant run in my place."

The King said, "Are you sure? My daughter is a very swift runner!"

The Prince waved his arm. "I'm not one bit concerned. My servant can just run in my place."

The next morning, you can guess who stood at the starting line. The runner—Corrín-Corrón. The Princess came to the starting line, the gun sounded, and they dashed off!

The Princess was a fast runner—but nowhere near so fast as Corrín-Corrón. He soon arrived at the distant mountain that was the half-way point of the race and started back. When he saw how far ahead he was, he thought he would sit down and rest. Then he noticed a shady bush nearby, so he stretched out in the shade. And he fell asleep!

While he was sleeping, the Princess came running along. She saw him, so she crept over and took off his shoes. She picked some sharp thorns from the bush and put them by his bare feet. Then she ran on.

But Escuchín-Escuchón was listening. He heard Corrín-Corrón snoring. So he went and told the shooter — Tirín-Tirón.

Tirín-Tirón climbed a tree and looked out across the valley. He saw Corrín-Corrón asleep, and he aimed his rifle carefully. *Pow!* He shot the very tip of the runner's ear and woke him up.

Corrín-Corrón jumped up — and he stepped right on the thorns. He danced around howling and holding his foot. But Tirín-Tirón just shot some more — *pow! pow! pow!* And he shot the thorns right out of his foot!

Corrín-Corrón ran on. He crossed the finish line just ahead of the princess.

The King said, "Well, that was the first test. Here is the second: You will have to guess the one very strange thing my daughter has about her person. If you can do that, you may marry her. But if you fail — it will cost you your life!"

The Prince walked off muttering to himself, "Oh, what can it be? Maybe she has six toes on her feet. Maybe she has a birthmark on her shoulder. What can it be?"

And the Princess was also unhappy, because she had taken a liking to the prince. She was beginning to

70

wish that she might marry him.

That evening she spoke to her servant, "I'm so sad! My father says the Prince has to guess the strange thing I have about me. No one could ever guess that!"

The servant said, "Oh, no! You mean he has to guess that you have..." And she said what it was. And who should be listening but Escuchín-Escuchón!

The next morning the Prince appeared before the King. First he tried all the other things you might guess. He said, "I think the Princess has six toes on her left foot."

The King laughed, "Six toes? Ha-ha-ha! That's not it!"

"Does she have a tattoo on her left elbow?!"

"A tattoo? Ho-ho-ho-ho!"

Then the Prince said what Escuchín-Escuchón had heard, "The Princess has a long hair growing out of the middle of her belly. It winds around and around her waist ten times! Then it coils up like a rose in the middle of her back!"

The King gasped, "How did you know that?"

And the Princess also gasped. But there was a smile in her eye, because that's exactly what she wanted to hear.

Still the King didn't want to lose his daughter. He begged, "Please, don't take my daughter. I'll give you anything. I'll give you all the gold you can carry!"

The Prince smiled. "Will you give me all the gold my servant can carry?"

"I'll give you all the gold anyone can carry!"

So the Prince went and talked to the strong man — Cargín-Cargón. He told him to make a big sack out of leather.

When the sack was finished, servants started carrying gold from the King's treasury and dumping it into the sack. A hundred servants brought all the gold they could carry, but Cargín-Cargón picked up the sack and spun it around his head. He laughed, "I think it's still empty. I don't feel anything in there!"

A hundred more servants brought all the gold they could carry. Cargín-Cargón smiled. "It's still so light! Don't you have any more?"

All the gold in the kingdom went into the sack. The only gold left was the King's own crown. The King lifted the crown from his head. Then he turned to the Prince. "Please. Let me keep my crown. You may marry the princess."

So the Prince and the Princess were married and they returned to his land, where he was now the King! And the Princess was the Queen. They lived happily for the rest of their lives.

And even though the story doesn't say for sure, I imagine the servants were happy too. Wouldn't you be happy if you could do what they could do?

About
The Stories

"Tell me a story!" It is a request made by children throughout the ages, in every language known to humankind. In the little Hispanic villages of northern New Mexico the children plead, "*Cuente me un cuento*," and the old ones have a folktale, a *cuento*, to fill the request.

The tale the children listen to probably came from Spain three or four hundred years ago. It arrived first in Mexico and then traveled north as Conquistadores and colonists entered New Mexico.

A New Mexican *cuento* may have a familiar ring to it. You might recognize it as very similar to a story you remember from *Grimm's Fairytales*. In it you'll find the kings and princesses common to folktales from many lands. But it will also be full of the customs and humor of life in New Mexico.

These ten *cuentos* are retold in English just as they have been performed for audiences all over New Mexico. Hopefully the reader will take the time to learn a few and tell them so that the cultural treasure of the *cuentos* and the ancient art of storytelling will be kept alive.

The Illustrator

Lucy Jelinek is an artist-designer who has worked in New Mexico since 1978. Her company, Santa Fe Pre-Print, is a graphic design firm specializing in publications. She also designed and illustrated Joe Hayes' second collection of stories, *Coyote &,* and his third collection *The Checker Playing Hound Dog.*

The Publisher

Mariposa Printing & Publishing was established in 1980. Our goal is to provide quality commercial printing to the Santa Fe community and to provide quality-crafted, limited edition publications in various literary fields.

Titles include *Opening,* by Malcolm Brown, *Sweet Salt,* a novel by Robert Mayer, and three titles by Joe Hayes: *The Day It Snowed Tortillas, Coyote &* and *The Checker Playing Hound Dog.*

Your comments and suggestions are appreciated. Contact Joe Mowrey, owner-production manager, Mariposa Printing & Publishing, 922 Baca Street, Santa Fe, New Mexico, (505) 988-5582.